MOMOTARO

Peach Boy

MOMOTARO

Peach Boy

Illustrations by George Suyeoka
Edited by Ruth Tabrah
Adapted from the original folktales by
Island Heritage

An Island Heritage Book

Produced and published by Island Heritage Limited
Norfolk Island, Australia

Library of Congress Catalog Number 72-86744
ISBN Trade 0-8348-3004-3
This edition first published in Japan

For the Island Heritage distributor in your area,
please write or phone:

Island Heritage Limited (USA)
Editorial Offices
1020 Auahi St. Bldg. 3
Honolulu, Hawaii 96814
Phone: (808) 531-5091
Cable: HAWAIIBOOK

Engraving, printing, and binding by
Dai Nippon Printing Co., (International) Ltd. Hong Kong

An Island Heritage Book

SPONSOR

This book has been created for Island children
of all ages, and is brought to you by the men
and women of the Bank of Hawaii in celebration
of their 75 years of service to the people of
Hawaii, and the Pacific.

For my wife Irene,
my daughter Mia and my son Genn.
To Nancy, Herb, and Bob.
And, especially to the children of Hawaii,
who I hope will experience the joys I felt as a child
reading Japanese folklore.

"Kane-ga naru!" exclaimed Ojii-san, still strong looking at forty. In his youth he had been a powerful samurai. Now, he lived a simple country life.

Obaa-san, his wife, sat opposite him on the tatami eating breakfast — tea, rice, miso soup.

"Kane-ga naru," she echoed. They sat quietly while the deep tones of the temple bell filled their childless house.

This day was like all the other days they had lived on this farm together. Many, many winters. Many, many dawns.

The gong's sound died. The house ached with quiet. It was so still they could hear the crinkling of the shoji windows. The rice-paper was drum tight from the night's cold. The sun, spilling its first rays over the mountains, relaxed the paper into tiny warming sounds.

Ojii-san put on his straw sandals and set off up the mountain to bring down the firewood he had cut the day before. He expected no more and no less from any day than this one: to set out for work at daybreak, and to return home as the gong sounded dusk. To eat rice, drink tea, rest at night on his mat and be grateful. He accepted his life as it was.

It was Obaa-san who could not, even at their age, give up the hope that someday they would have a child. She felt empty and lonely while tending the fire this morning. She felt empty and lonely while hanging out the heavy futon to air, and while picking her way over the frost-slippery rocks to the stream where she washed clothes.

It was dreary work scrubbing the heavy winter kimonos in the icy water. As usual she pretended that these were children's clothes. She rubbed the heavy kimonos on the flat washing rocks. Her arms and body moved to the rhythm of the rushing water. This morning the sound of the mountain brook was, more than ever, like a lullaby. She closed her eyes and began to dream.

"Ah!" The chill of the swirling winter

stream was gone. The water felt strangely warm and pleasant. She opened dazed eyes. The sun glinted on the wet rocks like the sun of springtime. Green shoots were everywhere. The air was mild. The world felt different.

"Ah!" she gasped. Floating down the stream towards her, swirling and bobbing, was a giant golden peach. Never had she seen a peach so enormous, so perfect.

Impulsively, Obaa-san waded out into the warming water. She began to croon, in a low soft voice.

"Distant waters are bitter
Near waters are sweet
Flee from the bitter
Come to the sweet"

The peach floated closer and closer until it nestled against her. "It cannot be!" she thought. "What good fortune!" Gathering the peach tenderly to her bosom, she carried it home.

Impatiently she waited for dusk, the sound of the temple bell, and her husband. "Ojii-san!" she called out. "I have been waiting long for your return!"

Puzzled, Ojii-san took off his warajis, washed his feet and came into the house.

"I have a surprise for you!" Obaa-san greeted him. She pointed, trembling, to the enormous peach.

"What did you have to trade for that? And at this season?" he demanded.

"I found it floating in the stream. I brought it home for you," she said. Her words and her face glowed with happiness.

"Then it is a blessing from the gods," said Ojii-san, smiling with her. "We will make a feast on it. Here — let us taste a piece!" He reached to cut the fruit with his knife and then paused, astounded.

The giant peach bulged visibly with round bursting ripeness. Along the cleft in the golden skin, the flesh began to pull apart.

Obaa-san gasped. Ojii-san stared in disbelief.

The two halves of the peach spread apart and a perfect, tiny baby boy appeared.

Tears of joy streamed down the faces of Obaa-san and Ojii-san. Their dream of a child of their own had come to pass.

First Ojii-san took the baby boy in his arms. Then Obaa-san did the same. Filled with happiness at his birth, they named him MOMOTARO — Peach Boy.

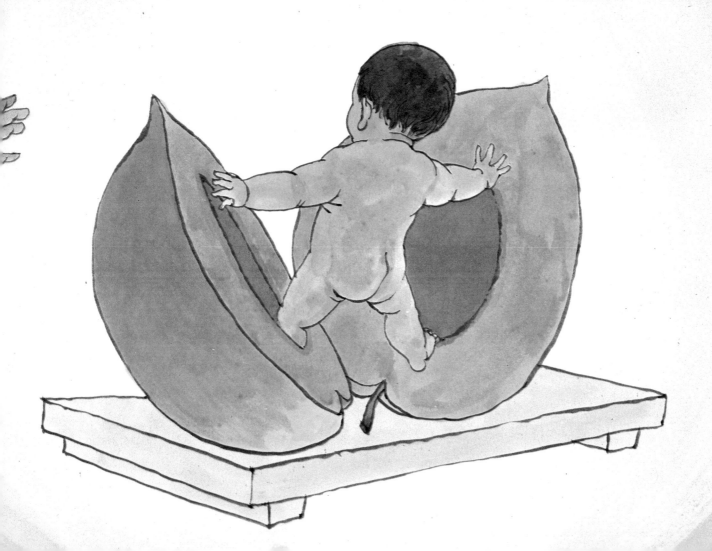

From that day, the temple gong sounded daybreak in a farmhouse filled with the happy noises of a child growing. Each day was a joy.

Harvest followed harvest.

The seasons quickly passed.

By the time he was seven, Momotaro shared in all the work of the village. He delighted in carrying the filled sacks of rice, one under a sturdy arm, a second on his shoulder.

"Ah! You are strong!" said Ojii-san.

When the time had come to learn the skills of a samurai, Momotaro was ready. He was a good student. His fame as a young samurai spread beyond the village. He was an expert horseman and a master archer. He never missed with katana, his sword, or yari, his spear. His parents regarded him with pride, tempered with sadness.

They sent the boy to the temple. There he studied the art of brush and ink and shū-shin, the way of the good life.

As he studied, one question bothered Momotaro. "Sensei!" he kept asking. "Who is it that comes to raid this village? Why is everyone so afraid? Why will none of you answer me?"

The answer did not come until Momotaro was fifteen.

On that day, Momotaro came to his parents and said, "Last night I had a dream. It was like a story Sensei told me. There was an island in the Inland Sea where monsters and evil ogres live. Sensei told me that for as many years as men can remember, these ogres have come to rob and torture and kill. Is this what you would not tell me about as I was growing up?" "Yes," said Ojii-san.

"In my dream I saw them!" said Momotaro. "They were coming to plunder our
village. Some were red. Some were blue.
The largest of all had pale skin with horns
and hairy legs."

"On my honor as a samurai," exclaimed
Momotaro, "those oni will never come to
our land again. Tomorrow I leave for the
Inland Sea. I will not return until they
are all destroyed!"

At once, his parents began to prepare kibi dango, a warrior's special food for Momotaro's journey.

Millet was brought out. The big wooden mortar was placed on the earthen kitchen floor. "Pet-ta-karo Pet-ta-karo," went the wooden pounder into the stickiness of the steamed grain.

When the millet cakes were ready, Momotaro's mother wrapped them in a bamboo skin and placed them in a flaxen pouch. Ojii-san helped lay out Momotaro's knife, his sword, his sash, his tessen-iron fan, — the garb of a samurai.

Then armed with all that he knew and all that he was, Momotaro set out.

Near the end of the first day he was hungry and thirsty. He followed a narrow rocky path to a small stream. No sooner had he taken a drink than a giant dog appeared.

The dog snarled, ready to lunge. "I guard this stream! No one drinks here without my permission!"

"Do you not know who I am, you arrogant beast?"

The dog stopped. "You must be Momotaro! Then that is Nippon ichi no kibi dango at your belt. Will you give me one?"

Momotaro reached into the pouch and broke a millet cake into two pieces. "I cannot give you a whole one, but I will share one with you. Will you come with me to fight the ogres?"

The dog ate the half millet cake. "All the animals of the forest know of your journey to battle the ogres, the evil oni. Watch what I can do with my strong jaws and sharp teeth to help you, Momotaro!" And with a single bite, the dog cut through a huge tree.

The next day, Momotaro and the giant dog rested at the edge of a bamboo forest.

A monkey dropped from the high branches, picked up Momotaro's fan, and began to run. In a flash, the giant dog leaped at the monkey.

"You are a thief!" Momotaro shouted. "I should let the dog tear you to pieces!"

The monkey did not tremble in the dog's grasp. "I was just testing to see if you are really Momotaro," said the monkey.

"I am," said the young samurai.

"Momotaro-san! Momotaro-san! What is in that bag at your waist? Could it be Nippon ichi no kibi dango? Give me one and I will join you!"

"I could use a clever fellow like you against the ogres," said Momotaro. "I cannot give you a whole millet cake, but I will share one with you."

After eating their kibi dango, Momotaro, the giant dog and the monkey set off together.

In the grassland beyond the bamboo, a brightly colored pheasant flew directly at Momotaro.

"You are a brave bird!" exclaimed the young warrior.

"Momotaro-san! Momotaro-san! What is in that bag you have at your waist? Could it be Nippon ichi no kibi dango? Give me one!"

"It is, but I cannot give you a whole one. I will share with you," said Momotaro.

"Are you going to let a mere bird join us?" growled the giant dog. The dog lunged at the bird. The pheasant whirred into the air, striking fearlessly at the dog with his sharp beak.

Momotaro watched the pheasant's bravery and daring. "Stop!" he commanded. "There will be harmony among us. Anyone who starts a quarrel will have to leave!"

He opened the bag and gave the pheasant a piece of millet cake. The four friends continued on their journey—Momotaro, the giant dog, the monkey and the bird.

Late that day they reached the shore
of the Inland Sea. Momotaro and his companions stared in dismay. Before them
spread a vast, heaving ocean.

"We will make camp here tonight," said
Momotaro quietly. "In the morning we
will build a boat." He passed a ration of
kibi dango to each one and ate a piece
himself.

At dawn the forest echoed with the sound of falling timber. As the trees fell, the giant dog's sharp teeth cut through the branches. The monkey tied the planks together with vines which the pheasant flew down from the mountainside. Late in the afternoon all was ready but the sail for the boat.

Momotaro said, "We will use our banner as a sail." Each took a corner and pulled. To their surprise the silken banner easily stretched into a great billowing sail.

For a day and a night Momotaro and his three companions sailed across the Inland Sea. Before dawn of the second day the pheasant soared above the ship to scan the horizon. Then he saw Ogre Island, the home of the dreaded oni. It rose dark and rocky out of a pounding surf.

Momotaro sailed the ship silently through the breakers.

"Fly to scout their stronghold before the sun is up and the ogres wake!" he ordered the pheasant.

Monkey leapt ashore and climbed the rock wall. Running to the heavy gate, he pulled back the locking bar from inside.

The gate swung open. Its rusted hinges screeched loudly.

The two sleeping oni guards woke at the sound. They grabbed their great iron clubs and began swinging wildly at Monkey and Momotaro. In a flash, the giant dog bit off the guards' heads.

Red, blue, and green ogres came running from every direction. With his katana, Momotaro warded off the attack. The dog snapped and chewed. The pheasant pecked at the ogres' eyes with his sharp beak while the monkey ran from wall to wall hurling rocks down on the ogres' heads.

The sleepy oni, certain that Momotaro's army must outnumber them, tried to escape. Momotaro, the dog, the pheasant and the monkey forced them off the cliff-top. They were dashed to pieces on the rocks below.

Only the chief of the ogres was left. He was the pale, hairy monster of Momotaro's dream.

Begging for his life, the oni chief unlocked the treasure room door.

"Spare me, oh Momotaro-san!" he cried as he wrenched off his horns, the source of his evil power.

The plunder of a thousand years crammed the treasure room. There was tortoise shell, pearl, coral, jade and a magic coat which made the wearer invisible. On a special chest was a wonderful mallet that could turn anything it struck into pure gold.

"We will use the swift ship of the oni to go back home!" said Momotaro. "The treasure and captive goes with us."

They spent weeks on the way home. The treasures stolen by the oni were returned to their owners. The pale oni chief, stripped of his power, withered away. At last Momotaro returned to his own village.

Obaa-san and Ojii-san came eagerly to welcome their son home. They could not restrain their tears of joy and pride.

Momotaro built a castle for the village with his portion of the unclaimed treasures.

For his brave companions the giant dog, the monkey, and the pheasant, he gave loyalty and protection.

And for his parents? He took tender care of them all the rest of their days.

An Introduction to Things Japanese

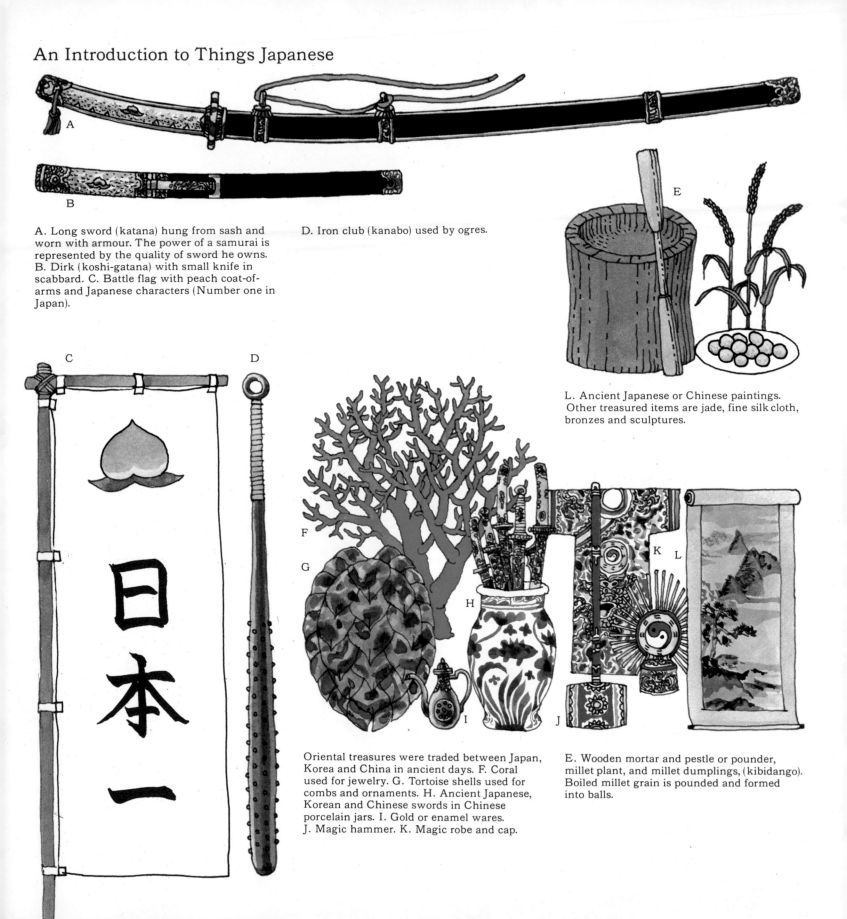

A. Long sword (katana) hung from sash and worn with armour. The power of a samurai is represented by the quality of sword he owns. B. Dirk (koshi-gatana) with small knife in scabbard. C. Battle flag with peach coat-of-arms and Japanese characters (Number one in Japan).

D. Iron club (kanabo) used by ogres.

L. Ancient Japanese or Chinese paintings. Other treasured items are jade, fine silk cloth, bronzes and sculptures.

Oriental treasures were traded between Japan, Korea and China in ancient days. F. Coral used for jewelry. G. Tortoise shells used for combs and ornaments. H. Ancient Japanese, Korean and Chinese swords in Chinese porcelain jars. I. Gold or enamel wares. J. Magic hammer. K. Magic robe and cap.

E. Wooden mortar and pestle or pounder, millet plant, and millet dumplings, (kibidango). Boiled millet grain is pounded and formed into balls.

日本一

Japanese armour is characterized by a flexible lamellar construction of small pieces of laquered iron strips tied together with leather or silk bindings. This gives the samurai the needed body protection and mobility lacking in heavy rigid European armour.

A. Bow, arrow and carrier. The grip on Japanese bows are below the center for ease in usage on horses.
B. Metal ribbed fan (tessen) capable of a painful blow.
C. Helmet (kabuto) with dragons head.
D. Shoulder and neck pad.
E. Iron strip lined arm sleeve.
F. Cuirass (do) or body armour.
G. Sash or belt.
H. Thigh pads.
I. Breeches (hakama).
J. Armoured shin guards.
K. Foot armour.
L. Swords.
M. Millet dumpling (kibidango) pouch.

Island Heritage is grateful to Dr. Hiroko Ikeda,
Dr. Barbara B. Smith, June Gutmanis, Judy
and Masahito Sato, Fumiyo Anematsu,
Dr. Esther C. Jenkins, and Dr. Hisao Kanaseki
of Tokyo University, whose knowledge and
aloha helped in the making of this book.

We are also grateful for the help of Gene Lewis
from Pacific Photo Type, Henk Kuiper of
Master Color Laboratories, Tony Kenyon,
and Yoshio Hayashi.

About the Artist

George Suyeoka was born and raised in Hawaii. A
McKinley High School student, he went on to
graduate in 1953 from the Art Institute of Chicago.

He is that rare combination in the world of art;
a fine artist, designer, illustrator, all at the same
time. His primary interest is in the fine arts
(drawing, painting, sculpture, & prints).

Married and with two children, he now lives and
works in the Chicago area with an office and studio
on Michigan Avenue.

Suyeoka's work has been published and exhibited
world-wide including the American Exhibit in Moscow,
Communication Arts Magazine, American Federa-
tion of Art Travelling Show, and numerous one man
exhibits.

In the field of illustration, his principal work has
been done for Scott Foresman and Company,
Encyclopedia Britanica, Harper & Row, Island Heritage, and others.